THE HISTORICAL RECORDS

OF THE

COMPONENTS OF CONRAIL

A Survey and Inventory

by

Duane P. Swanson

and

Hugh R. Gibb

Eleutherian Mills Historical Library

Greenville, Wilmington, Delaware

THE HISTORICAL RECORDS

OF THE

COMPONENTS OF CONRAIL

A Survey and Inventory

---

by

Duane P. Swanson

and

Hugh R. Gibb

Eleutherian Mills Historical Library

Greenville, Wilmington, Delaware

Copyright, 1978, by the
Eleutherian Mills-Hagley Foundation
Standard Book Number: 0-914650-17-3
Printed in the United States of America

CONTENTS

PREFACE

It is not often that concerned historians are
listened to when they sound the alarm bell. Here, however, we have one of those exceptions, the problem with
the successful solution. When in early 1976 Daniel J.
Collins and James O. Morris first voiced their appre-
hensions over the disappearance of valuable historical
railroad records, they had every reason to believe that
there would be the usual pattern of indifference or neglect.
To their amazement, and that of other interested persons,
it did not happen. The Federal Railroad Administration
came forth against destruction; Conrail pledged its cooperation; and the estates of those carriers now embodied
in Conrail displayed an enthusiasm not generally associated with dignified corporations. Last and most important,
the National Historical Publications and Records Commission provided the Ad Hoc Committee on National Railroad
Historical Preservation with the financial support for a
survey to locate, describe, and appraise those records.
By the time of publication many of the railroad
documents listed in this report could be located elsewhere. Although the survey team never anticipated such
a role, it found itself acting the part of the "honest broker"
in the proper disposition of those items that the estates no
longer needed or could no longer safely retain. These inventories are presented, we hope, in sufficient detail to
direct interested parties toward our third goal of appraisal.
A feeling of urgency was shared by all who were
involved in this undertaking. The creation of Conrail took
no one by surprise, but the pace of change that followed
its implementation on 1 April 1976 worried everyone.
Would there be anything left to examine? Our fears
proved groundless. The former carriers were not en-
gaged in a destruction program. In fact, some of the companies had been carefully depositing manuscripts and important imprints with responsible organizations for several
decades. We foresee this pattern continuing with the
estates.

It was not possible to visit every location where records might be stored. Still we believe that we have covered the important repositories and that the report is presented in such detail that it will be useful to the present owners and to future researchers. The complete inventories compiled by the field survey team and by various railroads and academic repositories, amounting to about 3500 pages, will remain on file at the Eleutherian Mills Historical Library. That institution will answer inquiries on specific collections.

The report provides information on two basic kinds of records, those held by the trustees of the estates of former carriers and those held by historical agencies, libraries, and other repositories. The former are under no obligation to provide access to those items listed in the inventories. It is to be hoped, however, that a ground swell of interest and inquiry will be generated and that this will encourage the present owners to place their archives in historical institutions.

That this survey would not have been possible without the cooperation of various agencies and individuals is self-evident. The surprising factor was the historical commitment displayed by all, a commitment that certainly lightened the work of the survey team. Let us offer due recognition.

Miss Minnie Dobes, Vice President-Finance to the Trustee of the Lehigh Valley Railroad, must be singled out for the enthusiasm she brought to the project. Her endeavors to preserve railroad records have been recognized for several decades and have resulted in the enrichment of historical collections belonging to the states of New Jersey and Pennsylvania.

Robert D. Timpany, Trustee of the Central Railroad Company of New Jersey, offered complete access to his files, both historical and current. His secretary, Janice Mackinac, guided us through the intricacies of those files.

In Cleveland, Milford M. Adams, Administrative Officer of the Erie Lackawanna Railway, not only made the company's historical records available but acted as a liaison with the local office of Conrail, which had inherited the current operating files. It was in Cleveland that the survey team received its most unusual assistance: eight students from Ruth Helmuth's archival class at Case Western Reserve University. In addition to gaining practical experience in inventorying the Erie Lackawanna papers, their efforts enabled the survey team to compress five days' work into three.

J. E. Berg, Secretary and Treasurer to the Trustee of the New York, New Haven, and Hartford Railroad, has been instrumental in placing the archives of the New Haven Railroad in repositories throughout New England. He welcomed the endeavors of the team and was most helpful in identifying the other repositories. Following his leads, we visited Richard Schimmelpfeng at the University of Connecticut and Mrs. Stuart M. Frank at Mystic Seaport, both of whom proved most helpful.

The George Arents Research Library at Syracuse University has a fine collection of Lackawanna, Erie, and New York Central records. Donald Anthony, Metod Milac, and Kenneth Oberempt all gave generously of their time and expertise.

W. Gifford Moore, former president of the Lehigh and Hudson River Railway and now the Special Consultant to its Trustee, traveled all the way from Washington, D. C., to Warwick, N. Y., to open the former headquarters building. Having the company's records in one location plus the availability of its top official to answer questions made for an ideal situation.

A. V. Martorelli, Assistant Secretary to the Trustee of the Penn Central Transportation Company, has a record of cooperation in historical matters that goes back several decades. Many graduate students are beholden to him for the successful completion of their theses. He fully appreciated our problems with regard to the enormous quantity of Pennsylvania and New York Central documents and gave us carte blanche. At this point it would be most appropriate to mention the aid we received at the huge Merion Warehouse in Philadelphia. Vincent Stamato and Hugh Meehan, with a small staff, operate what must be the largest railroad archive in the world. Conrail employees today, they were brought up in the tradition of the Pennsylvania Railroad and can offer instant retrieval from among 360,000 cubic feet of records.

At the time this survey was made much material was in the temporary custody of Conrail. It would have been impossible to conduct our survey without the cooperation of that agency. Our special thanks goes to William H. Couch, Conrail's Manager of Contracts and Records Management. Not only did he physically aid us in inventorying New York Central records, but he was also at the end of a telephone line if questions arose during our field surveys. Bill faithfully attended the meetings of the Ad Hoc Committee on National Railroad Historical Preservation. We were sorry to lose him to a well-earned retirement midway in our project. Fortunately, his successor, Thomas Judge, has carried on in the same tradition.

Much effort was saved by the inventories supplied at Syracuse University and Mystic Seaport. We were not able to visit the Baker Library at Harvard University, but its Curator of Manuscripts and Archives, Robert W. Lovett, furnished the details that completed the review of the New Haven Railroad.

To those bemused but helpful railroaders with whom we came in contact, our sincere thanks. We hope they will see this report and receive a vicarious satisfaction from it.

I.
THE HISTORY OF THE PROJECT

On 1 April 1976 seven eastern railroads were merged into the Consolidated Rail Corporation (Conrail). This was the largest merger of transportation companies ever effected in the United States and involved the following carriers:

Central Railroad Company of New Jersey
Erie Lackawanna Railway Company, a 17
   October 1960 merger of
     Erie Railroad Company
     Delaware, Lackawanna & Western
      Railroad Company
Lehigh and Hudson River Railway Company
Lehigh Valley Railroad Company
Penn Central Transportation Company, an
   8 May 1968 merger of
     Pennsylvania Railroad Company
     New York Central Railroad Company
     New York, New Haven & Hartford Railroad
      Company (entered merger 1 January 1969)
Pennsylvania - Reading Seashore Lines
Reading Company.

The physical plant and those records necessary for continued rail operations were conveyed to Conrail on that date. Real estate and records not required by Conrail remained the property of the estates of the former carriers, each administered by one or more trustees.

It was the records retained by the trustees of the former carriers that exercised two railroad historians, Daniel W. Collins, an official of the United Transportation Union, and James O. Morris, a professor in the New York State School of Industrial and Labor Relations. Long associates in a project to preserve railroad labor archives at Cornell University, they approached Daniel M. Collins,

Labor-Management Specialist with the Federal Railroad Administration, for assistance in preventing what they feared would be the destruction of valuable historical railroad manuscripts. Asaph H. Hall, Administrator, Federal Railroad Administration, was sympathetic and appointed Collins and Gregory L. Sutton, Research Analyst with the F.R.A., to form an Ad Hoc Committee on National Railroad Historical Preservation. The formation of the committee took place during late February and early March of 1976, and its first meeting was on 14 April 1976. The committee as originally constituted consisted of:

> Daniel M. Collins, Labor-Management Specialist, Federal Railroad Administration
> Daniel W. Collins, Assistant General Secretary and Treasurer, United Transportation Union
> Meyer H. Fishbein, Director, Military Archives Division, National Archives
> Hugh R. Gibb, Specialist in Industrial Collections, Eleutherian Mills Historical Library
> James O. Morris, Professor, New York State School of Industrial and Labor Relations
> Stephen Salsbury, Chairman, History Department, University of Delaware
> Gregory L. Sutton, Research Analyst, Federal Railroad Administration
> Richmond D. Williams, Director, Eleutherian Mills Historical Library.

When the Eleutherian Mills Historical Library was contacted by Mr. Sutton in February 1976, it conducted a preliminary investigation into the retention policies of Conrail and the former carriers. While both sides gave verbal assurances that none of the records were in immediate danger of destruction, something more binding was in order. Accordingly, at the first meeting of the committee, it was decided to ask an official of the United

States Department of Transportation to contact the various parties for written assurance that they would not destroy their records.

Mr. Hall undertook this task, and favorable replies were received from the Central of New Jersey, Lehigh Valley, Penn Central, and Reading railroads. Mr. Edward G. Jordan, chairman of Conrail, pledged the cooperation of his organization and appointed William H. Couch, Manager of Contracts and Records Management, to be Conrail's liaison person with the committee. Mr. Couch attended all subsequent meetings and became, in effect, an ex-officio member of the committee.

Random sampling of Lehigh Valley and Central of New Jersey records, done by Hugh Gibb from May to July of 1976, indicated that there was uncertainty as to the legal ownership of the non-operational records and that the volume involved was far beyond that envisioned by the committee. Accordingly, at the 13 July 1976 meeting, the committee voted to conduct a proper survey and to seek financial aid for the work. It was also decided that the survey should be conducted by the Eleutherian Mills Historical Library, a division of the Eleutherian Mills-Hagley Foundation.

Application was made on behalf of the Foundation to the National Historical Publications and Records Commission for a records program grant to enable the committee "to locate, appraise, and describe the historical records of the seven merged railroads; to test present methodology and guidelines for handling future Conrail acquisitions; and to create a permanent alliance of individuals and institutions willing to provide continuity and direction for these and future efforts to preserve railroad archives." The larger purpose of the committee was to preserve invaluable historical data from inadvertent or willful destruction. The grant was approved by NHPRC on 13 September 1976 to cover the period 18 October 1976 to 15 July 1977.

As soon as the grant became effective Richmond D. Williams selected Duane Swanson and Hugh Gibb to be the team to conduct the survey. Swanson, Field Representative for the Minnesota Historical Society, had considerable experience in dealing with railroad archives. At the time he was in charge of that institution's project for the preservation of the Great Northern Railway's records, having reduced its bulk from 500,000 to 15,000 linear feet of high-yield research material. Gibb's background included forty years of interest in railroad history and a decade of experience in acquiring and inventorying large industrial collections, including that of the Reading Company, for the Eleutherian Mills Historical Library.

II.
PLANNING FOR THE SURVEY

A plan of campaign was drawn up based on the pre-grant surveys and on Duane Swanson's valuable experience in handling unwieldy masses of records. Suitable reporting forms were adapted from those used by the Minnesota Historical Society. Most important was the schedule of visitations.

The team planned to be in the field one week of each month from November 1976 through April 1977. Only the New York State visits in December 1976 occupied an entire week, as the furnishing of inventories by certain repositories enabled the team to shorten its working time. In all, ten field trips were made, two after April 1977.

8-10 November 1976

Cleveland, Ohio, at the headquarters of the Erie Lackawanna Railway Company.

6-8 December 1976

Syracuse, N. Y. , at Syracuse University Library, for Erie, Lackawanna, and New York Central railroad records.

9-10 December 1976

New York, N. Y. , at Conrail Headquarters and the Williams Printing Company warehouse, for New York Central Railroad records.

11-14 January 1977

Philadelphia, Pa. , at Merion Warehouse, for Pennsylvania Railroad and New York Central Railroad records.

15-18 February 1977

Philadelphia, Pa. , at Merion Warehouse, for Pennsylvania Railroad and New York Central railroad records.

14-15 March 1977

Newark and Hoboken, N. J. , for Central of New Jersey, Erie, and Lackawanna railroad records.

18-19 April 1977

New Haven, Conn. , at the headquarters of the New York, New Haven & Hartford Railroad.

20-21 April 1977

Storrs and Mystic, Conn. , at University of Connecticut and Mystic Seaport, for New York, New Haven & Hartford railroad records.

13 September 1977

Hoboken, N. J. , at Hoboken Terminal, for Central of New Jersey, Erie Lackawanna, and Pennsylvania railroad records.

26 August 1978

Warwick, N. Y. , at the headquarters of the Lehigh & Hudson River Railway.

The actual survey went very smoothly. In all instances the team was shown the areas of storage and given unrestricted access to the records. There was no close supervision, but most storerooms had telephone connections and the answers to problems were never far away. Record survey data sheets were used to report each type and series of record. The raw data were then summarized on inventory sheets. The latter adhered, as closely as possible, to the guidelines established by the late Arthur Cole, professor at the Harvard Graduate School of Business. The survey inventories are actually a condensed version of these lists.

III.
THE SURVEY INVENTORIES

The results of our survey will be reported by carrier rather than by repository. The latter will be indicated by means of locational abbreviations such as Gateway One (GO), which will be explained in the "Locations Visited" section preceding each carrier's listing. The Penn Central and Erie Lackawanna mergers have been of such recent date that their major components will be treated as individual companies.

Because we are dealing with railroad records the basic organizational grouping is by department. The term used for a particular unit of a necessity varies, but volume (vol. or vols.) is the most common designation due to the predominance of minute books and accounting records. The term does not imply that all books are of equal size. However, a good conversion factor for nineteenth-century bound accounting volumes is four per linear foot; for minute books five per linear foot. Dates separated by a hyphen, i. e. (1900-1905), indicate the earliest and latest years for a particular series. They do not, however, indicate that the series is complete.

PENN CENTRAL TRANSPORTATION COMPANY

The largest carrier in this survey is the Penn Central Transportation Company, formed by a merger of the Pennsylvania Railroad Company and the New York Central Railroad Company on 8 May 1968. The merged company was originally known as the Pennsylvania New York Central Transportation Company. This cumbersome designation was changed to Penn Central Company and finally to Penn Central Transportation Company on 1 October 1969. The New York, New Haven & Hartford Railroad Company joined the Penn Central on 1 January 1969.

Many Penn Central records have been transferred to Conrail and to the National Railroad Passenger Corporation (Amtrak) for their operating purposes. The rest remain in the possession of the Trustees of the Penn Central Transportation Company and constitute important exhibits in the bankruptcy proceedings that have been in progress since 21 June 1970. The survey team did not examine Penn Central items. Rather, it confined its efforts to the three major companies absorbed in the merger.

PENNSYLVANIA RAILROAD COMPANY

Locations Visited

Offices of the Trustees of the Penn Central
Transportation Company, Industrial Valley
Bank Building, 17th and Market Streets,
Philadelphia, Pa. (IVB)

Merion Warehouse, 49th Street and Merion
Avenue, Philadelphia, Pa. (MW)

Mail Room, Erie Lackawanna Terminal,
Hoboken, N. J. (MR)

The main records center of the Pennsylvania Railroad was the Merion Warehouse. Until 1923 central storage was in vaults underneath the viaduct (Chinese Wall) west of Broad Street Station, Philadelphia. Following a fire in that year, when many records were destroyed by water damage, the railroad established the Merion Warehouse. Today this building is probably the largest railroad archive in the world, containing 360,000 cubic feet of material, most of it concerning the Pennsylvania Railroad. According to the current finding aids, Pennsylvania records are represented by 61,820 "permanent" items and 41,081 "temporary" items. The latter category refers to those things scheduled for limited retention periods. The others we may presume are to be retained forever. An "item" may be a single volume, a box, or a wrapped bundle. Most fall into the latter category.

The Merion Warehouse is now a Conrail property, which means that the Penn Central Trustees must eventually find new quarters for their retained records. There are rumors that a newer but smaller building will be acquired. It is hardly likely, therefore, that the present quantity of records will be retained, which could result in a major disposal problem. Hoboken Terminal also belongs to Conrail and presently seems to be a dumping ground for those items that Conrail does not want but hesitates to destroy. The Pennsylvania records at that location are mostly claims for violations of labor contracts in the New York Zone from 1930 to 1950.

Because of the quantities involved, it is physically impossible to produce even a detailed summary of extant Pennsylvania Railroad records. We are therefore presenting the Pennsylvania Railroad portion of this survey in the form of comments about the more significant parts of this vast collection.

Minute Books

The parent company minute books, complete from 1846 to 1958, are in the possession of the Secretary to the Trustees of the Penn Central, whose office is located at IVB. Legally they must remain in his custody. Microfilm copies through 1950, stored in the vaults of the Amtrak station at Lancaster, Pa., are available.

The books of the subsidiary companies (branch roads in Pennsylvania Railroad terminology) are at Merion Warehouse. Eight hundred eleven separate companies have been identified, but the number of volumes is not known as they are in wrapped packages. The oldest single item is Minute Book No. 1 of the New Castle and Frenchtown Turn Pike and Rail Road Company, which dates from 1830.

Presidential Correspondence

There is a limited amount of early presidential correspondence from the administrations of Samuel V. Merrick (1846-49) and William C. Patterson (1849-52). The volume of material increases with the presidency of J. Edgar Thomson (1852-74). The presidential files of Thomas Scott (1874-80) have not been found, but there is

material from his period as general manager. The
letters of George B. Roberts are missing, which is
unfortunate as the 1880-97 period was one of great
expansion in the system. Correspondence becomes
voluminous with Frank Thomson (1897-99) and re-
mains that way with Alexander J. Cassatt (1899-1907),
James McRea (1907-13), Samuel Rea (1913-25), W. W.
Atterbury (1925-35), and Martin W. Clement (1935-51).
There are special presidential files covering
the engineering and progress reports, with photographs,
of the Pennsylvania Tunnel and Terminal Project at
New York City (1902-10), as well as three trunks containing records from General Atterbury's service as
Director General of the Transportation of the American
Expeditionary Forces (1917-18). The amount of execu-
tive level correspondence preserved by the Pennsylvania
Railroad sets it apart from the other railroads in this
survey.

Chief of Motive Power - Motive Power Accountant

By combining the files of these two officers a
rather complete picture of motive power and rolling stock
can be gathered. Records, both historical and technical,
of equipment construction are supplemented by renumber-
ing and destruction lists. The parent company and the
major subsidiaries are represented, while Altoona Shop
records exist from 1866. Of particular interest is the ex-
perimental motive power never accepted for operation.
The Pennsylvania Railroad was the first interstate carrier
to adopt the all-steel passenger car and the development
files for this are found here.

Chief Engineers

The various chief engineers in the Eastern, Central, and Western Regions, and in the New York Zone
were, in effect, civil engineers responsible for all con-

struction and maintenance not directly applicable to on-track equipment. Existing construction contracts go back to No. 1, January 1862, at which time the company seems to have systematized its record keeping. All of the major construction projects are found in these files except the New York Tunnel project, which seems to have been handled at the presidential level.

Secretary

The bulk of the secretary's files consists of copies of the annual reports of the parent company and subsidiaries. These are obtainable elsewhere, mainly in the reference department of public libraries, but the collection at Merion is probably the most complete at any one location. Stock and bond registers constitute the other major category of materials in the secretary's files.

General Counsel

Legislative matters including relations with governmental agencies, at all levels, are in this province. Here are found leases, agreements, and abandonment proceedings. The correspondence relating to franchises and titles begins in 1855.

Comptroller

The early accounting records are found in the comptroller's files. The oldest volume is a ledger of the New Castle and Frenchtown Turn Pike and Rail Road Company (1830). The oldest "main line" record is a day book of the Harrisburg, Portsmouth, Mt. Joy and Lancaster Rail Road Company (1834). The Associates of the Jersey Company is actually the oldest Pennsylvania Railroad subsidiary (1804), but existing records do not start until 1839. The accounting records of all predecessors of the Pennsylvania-Reading Seashore Lines (pre-1933) went to the Pennsylvania Railroad. Thus one finds Camden & Atlantic and West Jersey & Seashore books at Merion. The Atlantic City Railroad, a Reading Company subsidiary, is also in this repository, not at the seemingly more logical Reading Terminal.

Engineer of Tests

The Pennsylvania Railroad was always "engineering oriented," and this attitude was manifested early in its history when a Department of Physical Tests was created at Altoona on 2 April 1874. On 1 November 1875 it was reorganized as the Department of Physical and Chemical Tests. Existing records date from 1903, when the first plant to test locomotives under simulated operating conditions was erected at the Altoona Works. Test records of various kinds of equipment and rail-related products, including the famous electric locomotive tests at Claymont, Delaware, have been preserved.

NEW YORK CENTRAL RAILROAD COMPANY

Locations Visited

Offices of the Trustees of the Penn Central
    Transportation Company, Industrial
    Valley Bank Building, 17th and Market
    Streets, Philadelphia, Pa. (IVB)

Merion Warehouse, 49th Street and
    Merion Avenue, Philadelphia, Pa. (MW)

George Arents Research Library, Syracuse
    University, Syracuse, N. Y. (SL)

Following the Penn Central merger, the New
York Central's minute books were moved to Philadelphia. The books of the parent company were sent to
the secretary's office, while the subsidiary company
volumes were placed in the Merion Warehouse. The
records go back to Minute Book No. 1 of the Mohawk
and Hudson Rail Road (1826).

For corporate items other than minute books
the most complete collection is to be found at Syracuse
University's George Arents Research Library. This
material was given to the University when its former
repository, the West Albany Enginehouse, was demol-
ished. The parent company's records begin in 1853
with the merger of the New York Central Railroad and
the Hudson River Railroad and extend to 1957. This
amounts to 530 linear feet. Subsidiary company records total 767 linear feet and are shelved alphabeti-
cally. All carriers existing prior to 1853 are placed
in the latter category.

President's Office

1. Correspondence of Alfred E. Perlman (1954-68), 15 cubic feet. MW.
2. Letterbooks (1877-1910), 21 vols. SL.

Secretary's Department

1. Minute books (1914-68). IVB. Microfilm copies through 1950 are stored at the Amtrak station in Lancaster, Pa.

Legal Department

1. Letterbooks (1910-26), 17 vols. SL.
2. Land and tax records (1856-1950), 13 vols. SL.

Treasurer's Department

1. Letterbooks (1853-71), 14 vols. SL.
2. Assistant Treasurer's statements (1922-25), 3 vols. SL.
3. Equipment trusts (1910-29), 9 vols. SL.
4. Stock ledgers (1853-1947), 202 vols. SL.
5. Stock dividend books (1854-1955), 92 vols. SL.
6. Stock transfers (1855-1953), 20 vols. SL.
7. Stock registers (1870-1922), 8 vols. SL.
8. Stock certificates (1853-1914), 27 vols. SL.
9. Bond ledgers (1868-1934), 10 vols. SL.
10. Bond journals (1874-1911), 6 vols. SL.
11. Bond registers (1853-1957), 54 vols. SL.
12. Other bond records (1853-1951), 53 vols. SL.

Comptroller's Department

1. Ledgers (1903-18), 2 vols. SL.
2. Cash books (1915-32), 78 vols. SL.
3. Paid vouchers (1915-27), 4 vols. SL.
4. Miscellaneous account books (1866-1940), 6 vols. SL.

New York Central Railroad Subsidiary Companies

(1826-1961)

      The New York Central's corporate structure included over 500 subsidiary companies. Minute books exist for 355 companies and accounting records for 310.

Secretary's Department

    1. Minute books
        (a) At Merion (1826-1950), 643 vols.
            (350 companies)
        (b) At Syracuse (1869-1961), 20 vols.
            (5 companies)
    2. Letter books (1840-1926), 279 vols. SL.

Legal Department

    1. Lease agreements (1853-1908), 4 vols. SL.
    2. Deed books (1887-89), 2 vols. SL.
    3. Tax records (1857-1910), 8 vols. SL.

Treasurer's Department

    1. Stock ledgers (1831-1942), 275 vols. SL.
    2. Stock dividend books (1837-1961), 335 vols. SL.
    3. Stock transfers (1826-1961), 392 vols. SL.
    4. Stock registers (1841-1938), 20 vols. SL.
    5. Stock certificates (1836-1961), 399 vols. SL.
    6. Stock subscription lists (1868-1961), 31 vols. SL.
    7. Bond ledgers (1860-1946), 89 vols. SL.
    8. Bond interest books (1849-1944), 68 vols. SL.
    9. Bond transfers (1859-1941), 82 vols. SL.
   10. Bond registers (1851-1931), 40 vols. SL.
   11. Bond certificates (1848-1934), 92 vols. SL.

Comptroller's Department

1. Journals (1866-1915), 39 vols. SL.
2. Ledgers (1865-1908), 105 vols. SL.
3. Cash books (1840-1932), 374 vols. SL.
4. Day books (1848-54), 7 vols. SL.
5. Voucher books (1847-1932), 40 vols. SL.
6. Payroll records (1883-1934), 8 vols. SL.
7. Trial balance books (1893-1908), 15 vols. SL.
8. Equipment registers (1883-1933), 14 vols. SL.

NEW YORK, NEW HAVEN & HARTFORD RAILROAD COMPANY

Locations Visited or Contacted

Office of the Trustee of the New Haven Railroad, 54 Meadow Street, New Haven, Conn. (MS)

Conrail Warehouse, in the Car Yards, New Haven, Conn. (CW)

Baker Library, Harvard Graduate School of Business Administration, Cambridge, Mass. (BL)

Wilbur Cross Library, University of Connecticut, Storrs, Conn. (WCL)

G. W. Blunt White Library, Mystic Seaport, Inc., Mystic, Conn. (GWBWL)

New Haven Railroad historical records are rather widely diffused as a result of the enlightened preservation policy followed by this carrier over the years. The records were given to various safe repositories on the basis of geographical relevance. The records of those companies which identified with the Boston area went to the Baker Library, the marine items to Mystic Seaport, and the balance to the University of Connecticut. The remainder, mainly legal items, were retained at the New Haven headquarters.

Secretary's Department

1. Minute books
   (a) Board of Directors
      1. At Meadow Street (1870-1961), 51 vols.

2. At Conrail warehouse (1872-1913),
10 vols. (copy)
(b) Stockholders (1872-1961), 8 vols. MS.
(c) Trustees (1935-47), 22 vols. MS.
(d) Various committees (1893-1968), 20 vols. MS.

2. Correspondence (1920-60), 183 standard file
drawers. MS.

Treasurer's Department

1. List of New Haven securities listed on New York
Stock Exchange (1893-1955), 1 vol. MS.
2. Bond ledgers (1912-32), 1 vol. MS.

Legal Department

1. Agreements and leases (1846-69), 1 vol. MS.
2. Unbound leases and agreements, 25 standard
file drawers. MS.
3. Deeds, 16 standard file drawers. MS.
4. Proxies (1950-61), 5 standard file drawers. MS.
5. Reorganization proceedings (1935-74), 37 vols. MS.
6. Correspondence concerning Penn Central merger
(1966-67), 9 standard file drawers. MS.
7. Supplements to charter compilation of 31 Jan. 1907,
2 vols. CW.

Comptroller's Department

1. Authority for expenditures (1918-19), 1 vol. CW.
2. Ex parte and per diem correspondence (1960-67),
3 standard file drawers. MS.

New York, New Haven & Hartford Railroad Subsidiary
Companies

(1802-1960)

The New York, New Haven & Hartford Railroad
Company was involved with various types of transportation.
In the various repositories it was possible to identify 107
steam railroads, 71 street and electric railways, 11 motor
coach companies, 26 steamboat companies, 2 canal companies, and 21 miscellaneous (nontransportation) companies. The following inventories will follow these subject
headings.

Steam Railroads

Secretary's Department

1. Minute books
    (a) 1837-1947, 164 vols. CW.
    (b) 1884-89, 5 vols. BL.

Legal Department

1. Leases (1880-98), 1 vol. BL.
2. Charters (1892), 4 vols. MS.
3. Bylaws of subsidiary companies current to 1960,
    2 vols. MS.
4. Deed files (1840-90), 5 standard file drawers. MS.
5. Document files (1900-20), 5 standard file drawers.
    MS.
6. Miscellaneous legal documents (1845-1920), 5 vols.
    CW.

Treasurer's Department

1. Journals
    (a) 1835-63, 4 vols. BL.

      (b) 1861-66, 1 vol. WCL.
2. Ledgers
      (a) 1840-72, 3 vols. BL.
      (b) 1866, 1 vol. WCL.
3. Cash books
      (a) 1838-72, 10 vols. BL.
      (b) 1881-93, 10 vols. WCL.
4. Blotters (1854-87), 5 vols. WCL.
5. Stock registers (1835-41). BL.
6. Stock ledgers (1901-58), 3 vols. MS.
7. Stock dividend ledger (1852-72), 1 vol. BL.
8. Stock transfers (1907-17), 2 vols. MS.
9. Stock certificates (1901-58), 14 vols. MS.
10. Bond registers (1907-47), 2 vols. MS.
11. Bond transfers (1907-58), 1 vol. MS.
12. Appraisal of personal property at stations
      (1 Mar. 1893), 2 vols. CW.

Comptroller's Department

1. Journals
      (a) 1835-1927, 58 vols. BL.
      (b) 1836-1937, 134 vols. WCL.
2. Ledgers
      (a) 1874-1910, 14 vols. BL.
      (b) 1836-1947, 115 vols. WCL.
3. Cash books
      (a) 1839-1910, 30 vols. BL.
      (b) 1840-1907, 248 vols. WCL.
4. Day books
      (a) 1850-1903, 6 vols. BL.
      (b) 1833-78, 15 vols. WCL.
5. Blotters
      (a) 1853-66, 1 vol. BL.
      (b) 1836-1905, 17 vols. WCL.
6. Waste books (1844-88), 28 vols. WCL.
7. Voucher registers (1857-1908), 4 vols. BL.
8. Vouchers (1879-1907). WCL.

9. Payroll records
   (a) 1844-1911, 20 vols. BL.
   (b) 1837-99, 43 vols. WCL.
10. Bills receivable and payable
    (a) 1835-66, 5 vols. BL.
    (b) 1849-98, 56 vols. WCL.
11. Receipts and earnings (1872-76), 10 vols. WCL.
12. Expenditures (1865-1913), 39 vols. WCL.
13. Freight and passenger balances (1904-08), 2 vols. BL.
14. Operating earnings and expenses (1899-1911), 3 vols.
    BL.
15. Trial balances
    (a) 1869-1924, 27 vols. BL.
    (b) 1848-1917, 28 vols. WCL.
16. Inventories (1877-97), 14 vols. WCL.
17. Transportation journals (1839-72), 20 vols. BL.
18. Transportation ledgers (1849-72), 9 vols. BL.

Street and Electric Railway Companies

Secretary's Department

1. Minute books
   (a) 1901-58, 5 vols. MS.
   (b) 1862-1939, 76 vols. CW.

Legal Department

1. Charters (1903-12), 5 vols. CW.

Treasurer's Department

1. Report by Day and Zimmerman to Connecticut
   Company on physical and financial status (1 Feb.
   1924), 1 vol. CW.

Motor Coach Companies

Secretary's Department

1. Minute books
   - (a) 1924-39, 5 vols. MS.
   - (b) 1923-39, 10 vols. CW.

Legal Department

1. Operational contracts with former street railway companies, (1925-28), 1 vol. CW.
2. Operational certificates (1925-28), 1 vol. CW.

Steamboat Companies

Secretary's Department

1. Minute books (1821-1938), 69 vols. CW.

Treasurer's Department

1. Stock transfers (1890-96), 1 vol. CW.
2. Insurance records (1907-17), 16 vols. CW.
3. Insurance accounts (1899-1915), 2 vols. GWBWL.
4. Stock dividend ledgers (1875-98), 2 vols. BL.
5. Stock certificates of Old Colony Steamboat Co. (1864-71), 1 vol. GWBWL.
6. Coupon bonds (1881), 2 vols. GWBWL.
7. Bond transfers (1880), 1 vol. GWBWL.

Comptroller's Department

1. Journals
   - (a) 1874-1907, 7 vols. BL.
   - (b) 1860-1904, 41 vols. GWBWL.
2. Ledgers
   - (a) 1874-1910, 14 vols. BL.
   - (b) 1885-1915, 20 vols. WCL.
   - (c) 1860-1937, 25 vols. GWBWL.

3. Cash books
   (a) 1897-1904, 2 vols. BL.
   (b) 1865-1917, 67 vols. WCL.
   (c) 1868-1901, 21 vols. GWBWL.
4. Day books (1866-93), 4 vols. WCL.
5. Vouchers
   (a) 1888-1921, 19 vols. WCL.
   (b) 1894-98, 6 vols. GWBWL.
6. Bills payable and receivable (1905-11), 4 vols.
   WCL.
7. Trial balances
   (a) 1862-1923, 23 vols. WCL.
   (b) 1874-89, 3 vols. GWBWL.
8. Payroll records (1887), 1 vol. GWBWL.
9. Invoices (1874-94), 24 vols. GWBWL.
10. Register of audited bills (1878-1904), 6 vols.
    GWBWL.
11. Bills collectible (1894-98), 1 vol. GWBWL.
12. Inventories (1897-1912), 5 vols. WCL.
13. Administrative expenses (1903-04), 1 vol. GWBWL.
14. Operating expenses (1898-1902), 1 vol. GWBWL.
15. Vessel account books (1866-86), 4 vols. GWBWL.

Canal Companies

Secretary's Department

1. Minute books (1823-36), 3 vols. CW.

Comptroller's Department

1. Cash books (1825-54), 1 vol. BL.
2. Day books (1825-28), 1 vol. BL.

Miscellaneous Companies

Secretary's Department

1. Minute books (1841-1964), 24 vols. CW.

2. Letter book of Proprietors For Erecting and Supporting of a Toll Bridge from New Haven to Fair Haven (1842-47), 1 vol. CW.

Comptroller's Department

Records of the Union Wharf Company
1. Journal (1802-90), 1 vol. BL.
2. Ledger (1802-88), 1 vol. BL.
3. Cash book (1887-90), 1 vol. BL.
4. Day book (1887-1910), 1 vol. BL.

PENNSYLVANIA-READING SEASHORE LINES

The Pennsylvania-Reading Seashore Lines was formed in 1933 by a merger of the Atlantic City Railroad (Reading Company) and the West Jersey & Seashore Railroad (Pennsylvania Railroad). The road's records were destroyed when a fire leveled the general offices in Camden, N. J., in 1975. Although an unknown quantity of pre-1933 records was destroyed, much had been previously transferred into storage by the parent companies. This material is now located at either the Merion Warehouse, Philadelphia, or the Eleutherian Mills Historical Library, Greenville, Del. The latter has the Atlantic City Railroad minutes (1889-1901).

THE CENTRAL RAILROAD COMPANY OF NEW JERSEY

Locations Visited

Office of the Trustee, Gateway One, Newark, N. J. (GO)

Mail Room, Erie-Lackawanna Terminal, Hoboken, N. J. (MR)

Eleutherian Mills Historical Library, Greenville, Del. (EMHL)

The items housed at Gateway One are the property of R. D. Timpany, trustee of the railroad, and are part of his current files. They do have, however, both current and future historical value. The records at the Erie-Lackawanna Terminal are those formerly kept at 1100 Raymond Blvd., Newark, N. J., and moved to make room for Conrail offices. The CNJ claims to have legally transferred the records to Conrail. Conrail questions the legality of the transfer, which leaves ownership in doubt. The records at the Eleutherian Mills Historical Library are part of Accession No. 1451 (Reading Company) and consist of daily operating correspondence (1876-86) of John E. Wootten during the period when the Philadelphia & Reading Railroad controlled the Jersey Central.

The lack of early minute or account books for this carrier was disappointing. The Jersey Central's history embraces about fifty predecessor and subsidiary companies going back to the Elizabeth & Somerville Rail Road of 1831. Apparently no one knows what happened to the early items.

28

Secretary's Department

1. Minute books
   (a) C. R. R. of N. J. (1925-67), 74 vols. GO.
   (b) Subsidiary companies (1888-1976), 24 vols.
       GO.
2. Correspondence, 5 standard file drawers. GO.

Legal Department

1. Right-of-way and property maps for valuation
   purposes, 7 map-case drawers. GO.
2. Current leases, 5 standard file drawers. GO.
3. Lease agreements and correspondence, 5
   standard file drawers. GO.
4. Miscellaneous property correspondence, 1
   standard file drawer. GO.
5. Abandonment correspondence, 1 standard
   file drawer. GO.
6. Reorganization proceedings, 9 standard file
   drawers. GO.
7. General correspondence
   (a) At GO, 5 standard file drawers (1960-76).
   (b) At MR, 250 cubic feet (1950-76).
8. Law books (1930-65), mostly Federal Reporter,
   Federal Digest, and Atlantic Digest, 355
   linear feet. MR.

Comptroller's Department

1. Authorities for expenditure (1960-76), 75 cubic
   feet. MR.
2. Miscellaneous accounting records (1940-76),
   425 cubic feet. MR.

Operating Departments

1. Correspondence
   (a) At EMHL, 9 linear feet (1876-86).
   (b) At MR, 50 cubic feet (1950-70).

ERIE LACKAWANNA RAILWAY COMPANY

The Erie Lackawanna Railway Company resulted from the merger on 17 October 1960 of the Erie Railroad Company and the Delaware, Lackawanna & Western Railroad Company. Most of the Erie Lackawanna records have become a part of the working files of Conrail. Those items retained by the company's trustees are in the Midland Building, Cleveland, Ohio. (MB)

Secretary's Department

1. Minute books
   (a) Trustees and officers (1972-75), 5 vols. MB.
   (b) Stockholders and executive committees (1968-72), 5 vols. MB.
2. Stock certificate issue book, 1 Apr. 1968, 1 vol. MB.
3. Correspondence (1965-70), 4 standard file drawers. MB.

Comptroller's Department

1. Journals (1966-74), 8 vols. MB.
2. Journal entries (1960-67, 1971-73), 14 linear feet. MB.
3. Expenses paid by drafts (1970-73), 1 binder. MB.
4. Injury claim drafts (1970-73), 1 binder. MB.
5. Audited vouchers (1968-74), 3 linear feet. MB.
6. Working papers for locomotive and train costs (1958-64), 1 envelope. MB.
7. General correspondence and tax records (1970-76), 11 cubic feet. MB.

Imprints

1. Annual reports to stockholders (1960-67), 8 vols. MB.
2. Annual reports to the Interstate Commerce Commission (1970-73), 6 linear feet. MB.

ERIE RAILROAD COMPANY

Locations Visited

Office of the Trustees, Midland Building,
Cleveland, Ohio (MB)

Mail Room, Erie Lackawanna Terminal,
Hoboken, N. J. (MR)

George Arents Research Library, Syracuse
University, Syracuse, N. Y. (SL)

The Erie Lackawanna Railway was another
carrier with a strong sense of historical preservation.
Many of the early Erie and Lackawanna records were
deposited at Syracuse University. Others have been
carefully preserved at the Midland Building. There
does not seem to be any particular rationale as to
location.

The Erie Railroad underwent four changes in
corporate title as a result of three receiverships.
Records have survived from each corporate period.

New York & Erie Rail Road Company, 1832-1861

Secretary's Department

1. Minute books
   (a) Board of directors (1832-61), 4 vols. MB.
   (b) Executive committee (1833-47), 1 vol. MB.

(c) Stock commissioners (1832-33), 1 vol. MB.

Legal Department

1. Land titles and mortgages (1832-1941), 7 vols. MB.
2. Agreements and leases (1832-1930), 4 vols. MB.
3. Contracts (1844-83), 6 vols. MB.

Comptroller's Department

1. Journals
    (a) At MB (1833-51), 3 vols.
    (b) At SL (1845-62), 8 vols.
2. Ledgers (1833-62), 6 vols. SL.

Imprints

1. Annual reports to stockholders (1835-61), 3 vols.
    MB.
2. Contracts, legislative acts and miscellaneous
    pamphlets (1845-57), 2 vols. MB.

Eric Railway Company, 1861-1878

Secretary's Department

1. Minute books
    (a) Board of directors (1861-80), 2 vols. MB.
    (b) Stockholders (1861-80), 4 vols. MB.
    (c) Executive committee (1861-75), 3 vols. MB.

Legal Department

1. Mortgages and agreements (1845-66), 1 vol. MB.

2. Contracts (1851-79), 3 vols. MB.
3. Reorganization proceedings (1875-79), 2 vols. MB.

Comptroller's Department

1. Journals (1862-79), 13 vols. MB.
2. Ledgers (1862-79), 11 vols. MB.

Imprints

1. Annual reports to stockholders (1863-76), 2 vols. MB.
2. Circulars, executive orders, etc. (1872-88), 1 vol. MB.
3. Scrapbook concerning the "Erie War" (1868), 1 vol. MB.
4. Report of James C. Spencer, referee in The People vs. Erie Ry. (1875-79), 5 vols. MB.

New York, Lake Erie & Western Railroad Company, 1878-1895

Secretary's Department

1. Minute books
   (a) Board of directors (1878-95), 2 vols. MB.
   (b) Executive committee (1878-93), 5 vols. MB.
   (c) Finance committee (1884-93), 2 vols. MB.

Legal Department

1. Reorganization proceedings (1893-95), 4 vols. MB.
2. Charters, mortgages, etc. (1880-95), 4 linear feet. MB.

Comptroller's Department

1. Journals (1874-98), 12 vols. MB.
2. Ledgers
   (a) At MB (1878-95), 3 vols.
   (b) At SL (1883-93), 2 vols.

Imprints

1. Annual reports to stockholders (1878-1904), 5 vols. MB.
2. Annotated bylaws and organization (1880), 1 vol. MB.
3. Erie System, A Statement of Organization and Operation (1886), 1 vol. MB.

Erie Railroad Company, 1895-1960

Secretary's Department

1. Minute books combining board of directors, stockholders, and executive committee (1935-68), 34 vols. MB.*
2. Bond transfers (1953-73), 1 linear foot. MB.
3. Mortgage bonds (1941-45), 3 vols. MB.

Legal Department

1. Certificates of incorporation and bylaws (1903-38), 8 vols. MB.
2. Mortgages (1895-1903), 3 vols. MB.
3. Equipment leases, agreements, and conditional sales (1917-30), 2 vols. MB.
4. Reorganization documents (1895-96, 1938-42), 11 vols. MB.

*Minutes 1895-1935 not located.

5. Claim files for loss and damage, personal injury, and workmen's compensation (1946-70), 1 vol. MB.
6. Correspondence (1950-75), approximately 400 cubic feet. MR.

Comptroller's Department

1. Journals (1895-1965), 48 vols. MB.
2. Ledgers (1896-1974), 66 vols. MB.
3. Income statements (1920-71), 7 vols. MB.
4. Balance sheets (1907-73), 46 bundles. MB.
5. Federal income tax returns and supporting data (1913-66), 1 linear foot. MB.

Operating Departments

1. Internal reports
    (a) Index of bridges and turntables (1937 and 1948), 1 vol. MB.
    (b) Locomotive and train costs (1949-50), 1 vol. MB.
    (c) Equipment destroyed, remodeled, rebuilt, or sold (1921-54), 26 vols. MB.
    (d) Locomotive and car mileage record (1922-68), 5 vols. MB.
    (e) Freight train, locomotive, and car performance (1920-51), 2 vols. MB.
    (f) Tonnage reports by division (1929-51), 1 vol. MB.

2. Reports to regulatory agencies
    (a) Annual reports to I. C. C. on freight service performance (1922-63), 22 vols. MB.
    (b) Annual reports to I. C. C. Bureau of Valuation (1918-29), 1 vol. MB.
    (c) Annual reports to state regulatory commissions (1955-72), 4 linear feet. MB.

      (d) Quarterly reports to the State of New York
           (1928-38), 1 vol. MB.

Imprints

1. Erie Railroad mortgages (1890-1920),
   1 linear foot. MB.
2. Miscellaneous extracts from the minutes and
   other historical data (1920-40), 1 vol. MB.
3. Corporate history by the valuation engineer
   (1915), 1 vol. MB.
4. George H. Minor, The Erie System, Organization and Corporate History, 1911, annotated
   to 1925, 1 vol. MB.

Erie Railroad Subsidiary Companies

(1838-1976)

      Eighty-seven subsidiary companies have been identified in the following records. Not all of them are represented at any one repository, although there are 76 of the companies in the holdings at Syracuse.

Secretary's Department

1. Minute books
   (a) Board of directors (1873-1976), 17 vols. MB.
   (b) Executive committees (1911-63), 2 vols. MB.

Comptroller's Department

1. Journals
   (a) At MB (1890-1974), 44 vols.
   (b) At SL (1838-1954), 76 vols.

2. Ledgers
   (a) At MB (1868-1974), 90 vols.
   (b) At SL (1853-1953), 78 vols.
3. Combined journal-ledgers (1916-46), 30 vols. SL.
4. Cash books
   (a) At MB (1869-74), 2 vols.
   (b) At SL (1866-87), 4 vols.
5. Day books (1838-71), 3 vols. SL.
6. Voucher registers
   (a) At MB (1948-75), 6 vols.
   (b) At SL (1888-1910), 2 vols.
7. Balance sheets
   (a) At MB (1887-1967), 34 vols.
   (b) At SL (1898-1901), 3 vols.
8. Income statements (1908-67), 6 linear feet. MB.
9. Payroll sheets (1908-74), 54 vols. MB.
10. Audited vouchers (1910-73), 59 vols. MB.

DELAWARE, LACKAWANNA & WESTERN RAILROAD COMPANY

Locations Visited

Office of the Trustees, Midland Building,
Cleveland, Ohio. (MB)

George Arents Research Library, Syracuse
University, Syracuse, N. Y. (SL)

Lackawanna records were originally kept at Hoboken. After the merger with the Erie Railroad Company in 1960, they were either moved to the Cleveland headquarters or deposited at Syracuse University. The latter has published a detailed pamphlet on its Lackawanna holdings, Manuscript Register Series Number 6, September 1964.

In contrast to the Erie, the Lackawanna had a stable financial history. Formed by an amalgamation of the Liggett's Gap Rail Road and the Delaware & Cobb's Gap Rail Road on 30 April 1853, its growth was mainly by absorption of subsidiary companies. The corporate structure remained essentially the same until the Erie Lackawanna merger.

Secretary's Department

1. Minute books
    (a) Board of managers (1849-1960), 24 vols. MB.*
    (b) Stockholders (1921-60), 3 vols. MB.
    (c) Various committees (1853-1960), 26 vols. MB.*

*Syracuse Library has incomplete sets with the same inclusive dates, 17 vols.

Legal Department

1. Letter books (1871-81), 6 vols. SL.
2. Incoming correspondence (1865-1943), 37 Hollinger boxes. SL.
3. Documents relating to the incorporation of the D. L. & W. and predecessor companies (1832-66), 5 vols. SL.
4. Miscellaneous contracts (1852-1956), 7 Hollinger boxes. SL.
5. Insurance contracts (pre-1960), 8 standard file drawers. MB.
6. I. C. C. hearings (1930-50), 13 Hollinger boxes. MB.
7. Equipment trusts
   (a) At MB (1946-59), 7 standard file drawers.
   (b) At SL (1938-48), 7 Hollinger boxes.

Land and Tax Department

1. Letter books (1898-1924), 7 vols. SL.
2. Tax registers (1885-1917), 28 vols. SL.
3. Tax returns (1884-1953), 52 Hollinger boxes. SL.

President's Office

1. Letter books (1854-1916), 116 vols. SL.
2. Incoming correspondence (1867-96), 308 Hollinger boxes. SL.

Department of Vice President-Labor

1. Incoming correspondence (1904-43), 35 Hollinger boxes. SL.
2. Claim correspondence (1943-60), 35 standard file drawers. MB.
3. Union agreements (1950-67), 6 standard file drawers. MB.

4. Proceedings of the National Mediation Board (1916-48), 24 Hollinger boxes. SL.

Treasurer's Department

1. Letter books (1851-1910), 67 vols. SL.
2. Incoming correspondence (1850-1912), 564 Hollinger boxes. SL.
3. Various stock and bond record books (1854-1948), 340 vols. SL.

Comptroller's Department

1. Journals
   (a) At MB (1893-1960), 9 vols.
   (b) At SL (1852-1957), 112 vols.
2. Ledgers
   (a) At MB (1852-1969), 19 vols.
   (b) At SL (1852-1956), 75 vols.
3. Cash books (1850-1957), 346 vols. SL.
4. Combined journal-ledgers (1852-1912), 16 vols. SL.
5. Authorities for expenditure (1899-1921), 15 vols. SL.
6. Voucher registers (1899-1956), 179 vols. SL.
7. Voucher files (1875-1904), 30 wooden chests. SL.

Coal Department

1. Sales registers (1890-1914), 21 vols. SL.
2. Construction records (1853-96), 1 vol. SL.

Engineering Department

1. Accounts and accounting reports
   (a) Analyses of construction (1843-1918), 20 vols. SL.

(b) Analyses of renewal funds (1855-1900), 2 vols. SL.
(c) Analyses of additions and betterments (1882-1918), 5 vols. SL.
(d) Analyses of investments in leased lines (1907-18), 2 vols. SL.
(e) Analyses of charges in roadway (1854-1918), 2 vols. SL.
2. Items charged to construction (1842-1910), 3 vols. SL.
3. Property registers (1889-1946), 12 vols. SL.
4. Equipment and rolling stock registers (1850-1915), 5 vols. SL.
5. Investment detail in road and equipment (1915-35), 28 vols. SL.
6. Miscellaneous construction records (1853-1910), 15 vols. SL.

Operating Departments

1. Transportation expense files (1882-98), 44 Hollinger boxes. SL.
2. Registers of operating expenses (1885-1925), 21 vols. SL.
3. Miscellaneous operating reports (1856-1916), 38 Hollinger boxes and 37 vols. SL.
4. Reports to regulatory agencies
(a) Reports to I. C. C. (1888-1960), 16 Hollinger boxes and 32 vols. SL.
(b) Reports to the State of New Jersey (1877-1953), 101 vols. SL.
(c) Reports to the State of New York (1883-1959), 15 Hollinger boxes and 77 vols. SL.
(d) Reports to the State of Pennsylvania (1877-1960), 6 Hollinger boxes and 76 vols. SL.

Imprints

1. Annual reports to stockholders (1854-1960), SL. *
2. Corporate history, n.d., 4 vols. MB.
3. The Railroad Employee (house organ) (1891-1916), 3 vols. SL.

Photographs

At the Syracuse Library there are approximately 15,000 Eastman glass negatives (1865-1925) of scenes of motive power, rolling stock, right-of-way, and other property.

Delaware, Lackawanna & Western Railroad Subsidiary Companies

(1828-1976)

Secretary's Department

1. Minute books, board of directors
   (a) At MB (1875-1976), 35 vols.
   (b) At SL (1835-1946), 109 vols.
2. Charters, laws, and leases (1828-86), 1 vol. SL.

Comptroller's Department

1. Journals
   (a) At MB (1938-74), 10 vols.
   (b) At SL (1838-1950), 94 vols.

*Incomplete set at MB.

2. Ledgers
   (a) At MB (1869-1974), 14 vols.
   (b) At SL (1840-1950), 149 vols.
3. Combined journal-ledgers (1866-1935),
      5 vols. SL.
4. Cash books (1850-1936), 35 vols. SL.
5. Day books (1857-75), 2 vols. SL.
6. Voucher registers
   (a) At MB (1963-68), 1 vol.
   (b) At SL (1880-1953), 57 vols.
7. Audited vouchers
   (a) At MB (1956-69), 5 vols.
   (b) At SL (1880-98), 2 Hollinger boxes.
8. Other accounting volumes
   (a) At MB (1898-1958), 18 vols.
   (b) At SL (1845-1961), 259 vols.

Engineering Department

1. Construction voucher files (1835-99),
      23 Hollinger boxes. SL. *

Reports to Regulatory Agencies

1. Reports to I. C. C. (1888-1946), 431 vols. SL.
2. Reports to state agencies (1880-1946),
      1,021 vols. SL.

* The records of the Morris and Essex Rail Road company consist of 383 volumes and 43 Hollinger boxes which are the most complete set of material of any Lackawanna subsidiary.

LEHIGH VALLEY RAILROAD COMPANY

Locations Visited

Office of the Trustee, Bethlehem, Pa.

Lehigh Valley Railroad Shop Building,
Packerton, Pa.

When this survey was first undertaken, the
Lehigh Valley Railroad's records were located at the
Office of the Trustee (former General Offices) at
Bethlehem, Pa., and in a former shop building at
Packerton, Pa. Since the trustee wished to dispose
of the records to a responsible repository as soon
as possible, an approach was made to the archival
authorities of the states of New Jersey and Pennsylvania.

Both parties accepted. It was agreed that
New Jersey would receive the records of the Morris
Canal and Banking Company and such railroad subsidiaries as operated within that state. Most prom-
inent among the latter are the Easton & Amboy Railroad Company, the Lehigh Valley Transportation
Company, and the National Docks Railway Company.
The remainder of the records went to the Pennsylvania Historical and Museum Commission. As with
other carriers, the minute books of the parent company, the Lehigh Valley Railroad Company, have been
retained by the trustee.

Present Location of Records

State of New Jersey, State Library, Trenton,
N. J. (NJ)

Pennsylvania Historical & Museum Commission, William Penn Memorial Museum & Archives Building, Harrisburg, Pa. (PHMC)

Comptroller's Department

1. Journals (1866-1919), 33 vols. PHMC.
2. Ledgers (1855-1938), 198 vols. PHMC.
3. Cash books (1855-1938), 47 vols. PHMC.
4. Balance sheets (1874-1918), PHMC.
5. Other accounting records (1862-1939), 102 vols. PHMC.

Lehigh Valley Railroad Subsidiary Companies

(1836-1940)

Secretary's Department

1. Minute books, board of directors (1836-1940), 186 vols. PHMC.

Legal Department

1. Mine lease books (1889-1928), 3 vols. PHMC.
2. Articles of association (1891), 4 vols. PHMC.

Comptroller's Department

1. Journals
   (a) At PHMC (1857-1940), 82 vols.
   (b) At NJ   (1871-1933), 36 vols.
2. Ledgers
   (a) At PHMC (1839-1940), 118 vols.
   (b) At NJ   (1865-1930), 45 vols.

3. Cash books
   (a) At PHMC (1851-1943), 43 vols.
   (b) At NJ   (1871-1904), 11 vols.
4. Day books
   (a) At PHMC (1852-87), 24 vols.
   (b) At NJ   (1880-98), 4 vols.
5. Voucher registers
   (a) At PHMC (1886-97), 2 vols.
   (b) At NJ   (1889-1901), 2 vols.
6. Balance sheets
   (a) At PHMC (1875-1901), 4 vols.
   (b) At NJ   (1891-1922), 13 vols.
7. Other accounting records
   (a) At PHMC (1867-1915), 16 vols.
   (b) At NJ   (1893-1932), 18 vols.

READING COMPANY

Locations Visited or Contacted

Office of the Trustees of the Reading Company,
One Plymouth Meeting, Plymouth Meeting, Pa.
(PM)

Reading Terminal, 12th and Market Streets,
Philadelphia, Pa. (RT)

Eleutherian Mills Historical Library,
Greenville, Del. (EMHL)

The Eleutherian Mills Historical Library is
currently the major repository for Reading Company
historical records. It has two collections, Accession
No. 1451 on deposit from the Historical Society of
Pennsylvania and Accession No. 1520 on deposit from
the Reading Company. For the purposes of this report, the two will be treated as one collection.

The Reading Terminal, still owned by the
trustees, is occupied by Conrail and the Southeastern
Pennsylvania Transportation Authority (SEPTA).
There are records stored at that location belonging
to the trustees, the disposition of which has not been
determined. The minute books of the parent company
have been retained by the trustees at Plymouth Meeting.

Unless otherwise noted, all Reading Company
records listed below are located at the Eleutherian
Mills Historical Library.

Secretary's Department

1. Minute books
   (a) Philadelphia & Reading Railroad (1833-96), PM.
   (b) Philadelphia & Reading Railway (1896-1924), PM.
   (c) Reading Company (1924-76), PM.

Engineering Department

1. Letterbooks (1865-1940), approximately 2500 linear feet. RT.

Treasurer's Department

1. Stock ledgers (1870-87), 1 vol.
2. Employees' bonding register (1883-90), 5 vols.

Comptroller's Department

1. Journals (1855-1917), 67 vols.
2. Ledgers (1835-1920), 138 vols.
3. Cash books (1895-1907), 3 vols.
4. Voucher records (1836-1914), 15 vols.
5. Payroll records (1848-1910), 27 vols.
6. Notes payable and receivable (1874-79), 1 vol.
7. Purchasing and receiving records (1890-1917), 9 vols.
8. Trial balances (1888-1926), 9 vols.

Transportation Departments

1. Agents' circulars (1876-1919), 51 vols.
2. Passenger traffic reports (1855-1912), 18 vols.
3. Records of passes issued (1869-1916), 92 vols.

Correspondence

1. Letter books (1844-1918), 549 vols. This
    represents the outbound correspondence
    of various officials. The bulk, however,
    comprises the files of the following four
    men:

    Gustavus A. Nicolls, vice president
    (1844-77), 87 vols.
    John E. Wootten, general superintendent
    and general manager (1865-86), 117 vols.
    Angus A. McLeod, general manager, vice
    president, and president (1886-93), 39
    vols.
    Theodore Voorhees (1893-1914), 220 vols.
    Voorhees served as both first vice presi-
    dent and president, but there are no
    presidential papers in the collection.

2. Inbound correspondence (1844-1920), approxi-
    mately 300 linear feet. A total of 105 of-
    ficials have been identified, but again the
    bulk of the correspondence relates to the
    four men mentioned above.

    Gustavus A. Nicolls (1841-86), 7 linear feet.
    John E. Wootten (1865-86), 49 linear feet.
    Angus A. McLeod (1886-93), 15 linear feet.
    Theodore Voorhees (1893-1915), 52 linear feet.

Miscellaneous

1. Photographs. There are 5,763 photographs,
    most of which concern major engineering
    projects in the Philadelphia area (1896-1912).

2. Statistical reports, various departments
    (1843-1919), 11 vols.

3. Board of directors, meeting agenda (1946-63), 11 cubic feet.
4. Files concerning the third reorganization of the Philadelphia & Reading Railroad (1895-1902), 3 linear feet.
5. Files concerning the construction and operation of Reading Terminal, Philadelphia (1887-1907), 3 linear feet.
6. Pamphlets. The collection of pamphlets (1870-1910) contains mostly the speeches of George Baer and Franklin Gowen, presidents of the Reading. 1 cubic foot.

Reading Company Subsidiary Companies

(1792-1958)

The Reading Company was involved in various types of transportation. It was possible to identify 110 steam railroads, 6 street and electric railways, 2 motor coach companies, 4 canal companies, 2 turnpike companies, and 18 miscellaneous (non-transportation) companies. The following inventories will use these subject headings.

Steam Railroads

Secretary's Department

1. Minute books (1829-1953), 165 vols.

Legal Department

1. Charters, contracts, and other legal papers filed by subsidiary road (1830-1950), 22 linear feet.

Comptroller's Department

1. Journals (1845-71), 4 vols.
2. Ledgers (1830-70), 4 vols.
3. Bills payable (1863-67), 1 vol.
4. Construction and maintenance records (1854-58), 2 vols.
5. Check stub books (1870-74), 2 vols.
6. Trial balances (1920-26), 18 vols.

Street and Electric Railways

Secretary's Department

1. Minute books (1892-1923), 6 vols.

Motor Coach Companies

Secretary's Department

1. Minute books (1924-45), 2 vols.

Ferry Companies

Secretary's Department

1. Minute books (1861-1938), 5 vols.

Comptroller's Department

1. Journal (1902-12), 1 vol.
2. Cash book (1917-23), 1 vol.
3. Voucher records (1922-23), 1 vol.

Canal Companies

Secretary's Department

1. Minute books (1792-1875), 10 vols.

Comptroller's Department

    1.   Journals (1816-48), 9 vols.
    2.   Ledgers (1816-85), 12 vols.

Turnpike Companies

Secretary's Department

    1.   Minute books (1795-96, 1853-54), 2 vols.

Miscellaneous Companies

Secretary's Department

    1.   Minute books (1848-56), 19 vols.

Comptroller's Department

    1.   Ledger (1880-81), 1 vol.
    2.   Voucher records (1914-18), 1 vol.

LEHIGH AND HUDSON RIVER RAILWAY COMPANY

Locations Visited

General Office Building, Warwick, N. Y. (LHR)

The Lehigh and Hudson River Railway Company was formed on 1 April 1882 by a merger of the Lehigh and Hudson River Railroad Company, the Pequest and Walkill Railroad Company, and the Warwick Valley Railroad Company. Following the opening of the Poughkeepsie Bridge in December 1888, the Lehigh and Hudson River became an important segment of the through route from the anthracite coal fields to New England. All records are currently housed at Warwick, N. Y.

Accounting Records (Auditor or Comptroller's Departments)

1. Journals (1882-1955), 18 vols.
2. Ledgers (1882-1956), 32 vols.
3. Cash books (1953-64), 11 vols.
4. Voucher registers (1927-63), 5 vols.
5. Cash vouchers (1934-65), 13 vols.
6. Audited vouchers (1941-50), 8 vols.
7. Payroll records (1909-64), 31 vols.
8. Detail of operating expense (1940-63), 21 vols.
9. Detail of investment in physical property and equipment (1918-20), 1 vol.
10. Balance sheets, income statements, and trial balances (1933-56), 19 vols.

Secretary's Department

1. Annual reports to the Interstate Commerce Commission (1916-64), 49 vols.

Traffic Department

1. Traffic sheets (1956-71), 14 vols.

Operating Department

1. OS (movement) reports (1926-32), 15 vols.

Official correspondence

The letter books of various officials (1938-69), are contained in 27 boxes and 37 binders.

IV.

CONCLUDING REMARKS

It is the sincere hope of all persons associated with this undertaking that we have established a new cause; namely, to encourage the railroad industry to set its historical house in order. This survey was conceived in a state of panic and carried out under geographical and temporal limitations. The degree of its acceptance should be the guide to the usefulness of further endeavors along these lines. Spatial costs of storage already indicate that time is running out for the carriers who wish to preserve their archives. Our appeal to them is to plan ahead and do it now!

5211